Just Be a Tree

© Copyright 2025-Alexis Crawford

All rights reserved. Permission is granted to copy or reprint portions for any noncommercial use, except they may not be posted online without permission.

Wyatt & Sons Publishers books may be ordered through booksellers or by contacting:

Wyatt & Sons Publishers, LLC
Mobile, Alabama 36695
www.wyattpublishing.com
editor@wyattpublishing.com

Because of the dynamic nature of the Internet, any web address or links contained in this book may have changed since publication and may no longer be valid.

Illustrations by: Kathy Caldwell
Cover illustration by: Kathy Caldwell
Cover design by: Mark Wyatt
Interior design by: Mark Wyatt

ISBN 13:978-1-954798-32-8
Printed in the United States of America

Just Be a Tree

by
Alexis Crawford

WYATT & SONS
PUBLISHERS, LLC

Mobile, Alabama

Introduction

Just Be A Tree is a simple, yet powerful parable for such a time as this. It tells the story of faith, trust, obedience, joy, fear, doubt, pain, humbleness, and sacrifice...but most of all, God's unconditional love.

The author is Jesus who spoke it through the Holy Spirit, to one of God's vessels, who then wrote the spoken words. It describes just one of God's creatures from birth through life's journey as an example of a child of God, living life as God created him to be, following God's plan and ultimately fulfilling God's purpose for his life, using a simple tree as an analogy.

As you read this story, please imagine it as if Jesus Himself were standing here reading it to you. It is His story and He is giving the world one more parable as a last minute "Hail Mary", to reach lost souls, restore Prodigals, and to remind all children of God that he created them to accomplish His plans and fulfill His ultimate purpose for each individual life.

1

Whew, it feels so good to be released from that dark, small shell thing. I can stretch a little now. Wait! What's that? I see some light up above me, I think if I stretch really hard, I can find it. Wow, I broke through a hard surface into a warm, bright light…I like it here, I feel free and so peaceful.

A few weeks have passed, and I seem to be getting taller. I wonder what I am supposed to do here other than just stand here. That evening, I saw the most beautiful colors in the sky, as I looked up in wonder, I heard the softest voice ever, yet it had my full attention.

"You are my creation; I am your creator. A tree is what I have created you to be. You will accomplish many functions, most all of them pleasant, you will fulfill my plans for your life to bring about my purpose. You need not fear what is to come or question what to do, just be a tree. I will always be with you and show you all things." "What shall I call you," I asked, "I am your creator and Father", he replied.

I am much taller now, with branches that always reach up giving thanks to my creator for what He made me. I spend my days doing what trees do. I love watching the squirrels play hide and seek in my branches. It sort of tickles when they run and jump on me. They also make nests in which to sleep and stay dry and warm. Speaking of nests, another favorite is the birds that build their nests in my branches. I wait patiently for the baby birds to break out of their shells, it reminds me of the day I broke out of my dark place. I rejoice and thank my creator every time I think back on that glorious day.

Another purpose I serve is to provide soothing shade for animals and strange looking animals, that my creator calls people. I think they look a bit like a tree. However, they only have four branches, two they move around on and two they do so many other fun things. I questioned my creator about being able to be more like them, to be able to move and do so many fun things. He asked me if I was happy with being a tree, of course I said "Yes". He told me he creates every different being to be what he created them to be, to fulfill his plans for them and his purpose. If they stray far from his plan, they will no longer be happy and will fall into sad, even scary darkness. "Oh no, I said, I don't want to go back to that place ever again." I'll just be the best tree I can be.

I'm not sure exactly how long it's been since that conversation, but one day I noticed these odd shaped, colorful things growing from my branches. As always when I have questions, I asked my creator about them. He told me they are flowers and will soon become fruit for all his created beings to eat and enjoy, (they smell amazing). He also said that only the trees that are faithful in being what he created them to be will produce fruit.

"Father, thank you for creating me to be a tree, I am happy and content just being a tree."

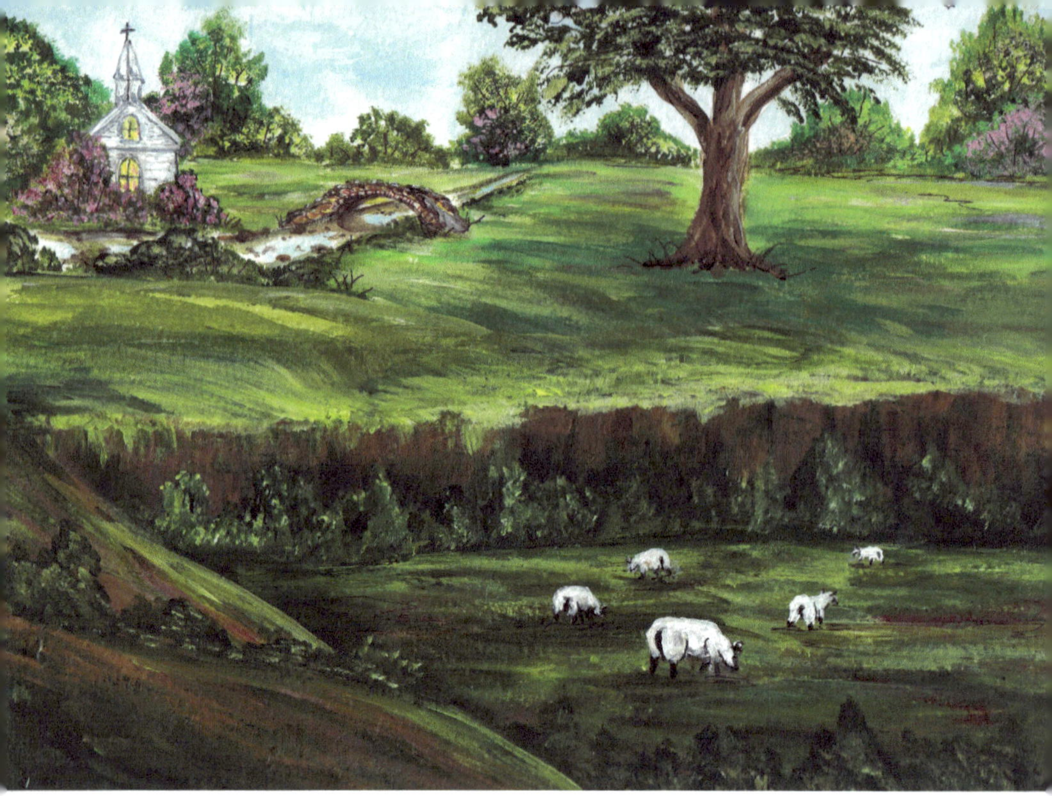

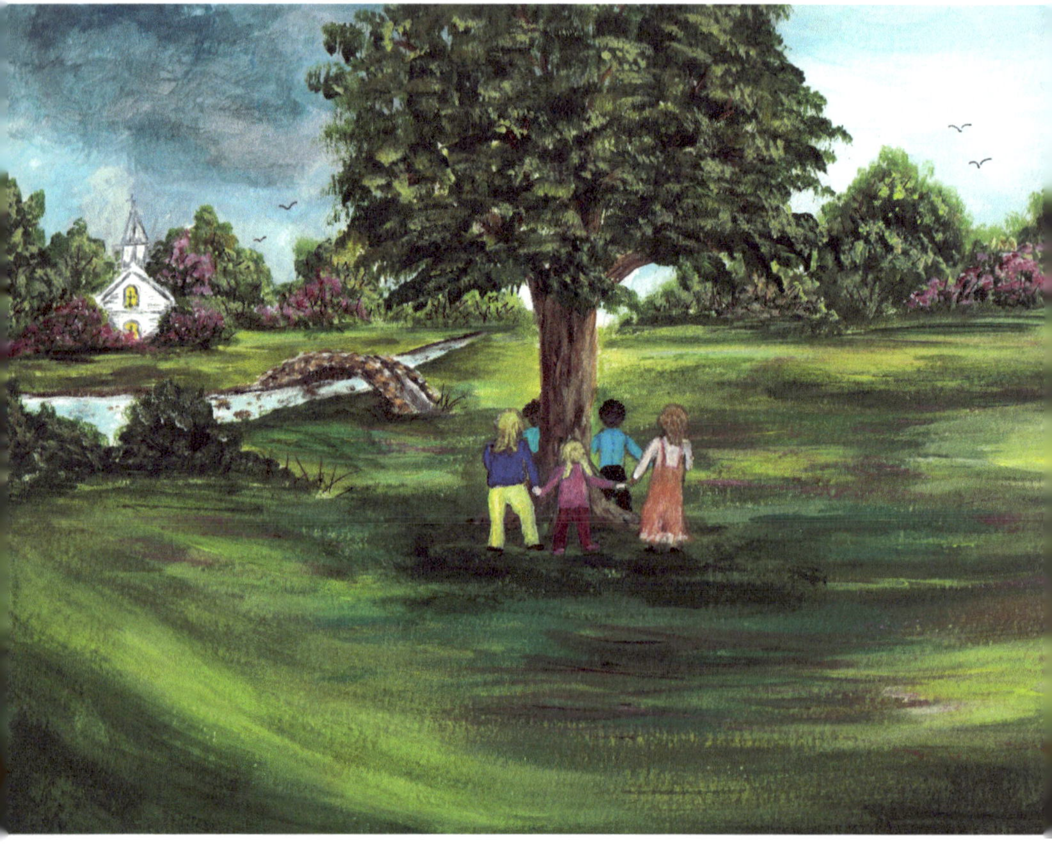

2

I should probably tell you about the place the creator planted me in. I am near a small brook that bubbles over the rocks, it always sounds so happy. There are many other trees, bushes, and flowers. We are on top of a hill, and I can see down into a beautiful valley that's full of the creator's animals. I watch them play and eat all that the creator has provided. There is also a small church on this hill. I love it when it's full of people. I can hear them singing to our Father and see them dancing to the music. When the wind blows gently, my branches sway with the music also. I feel like I am also thanking my Father for who He is and for giving me such an amazing place to live. I think it is the perfect place to live.

One day as the people were at the church the children came out to play. They joined hands and circled round me singing. It was glorious! The wind was blowing, and my branches were swaying over the children. It was the best day ever. However, the wind started blowing harder, it was causing my branches to bend so much it was painful. The sky turned dark, there were streaks of light shooting across the black sky and then a scary loud noise. There were huge drops of water falling from the sky so hard it was tearing through my leaves. The children ran into the church to get away from it.

The wind kept blowing harder and it was breaking off some of my branches; it was hurting, and I was scared. I cried out to my creator for help. "Father, what is happening, make it stop, I'm scared and I'm hurting, where are you, I asked?"

It seemed like a long time before he answered me. He finally replied, "Remember my precious little tree when I first spoke to you? This is a storm; they happen throughout every creation's life. They bring about my testing to see if you trust me even when things are difficult." Remember, I said you need not fear what comes, as I am always with you even if it seems I'm not. In the middle of the storm, don't look at the storm, as that brings fear, continue to focus on my presence and trust I will bring you through it."

"Father, the storm broke off some of my branches and it hurts. Will I hurt and look ugly forever?" "My precious, little tree, wait, keep trusting me and you will see my plan."

Just Be a Tree

It seemed a long time that I kept hurting, I would talk with my father every day and he encouraged me to trust and wait. One day I noticed I didn't hurt as much, and I also noticed small green sprigs growing where I was missing old branches. I was so excited. My father continued to ask me to trust and wait. Each day I saw new sprigs that were growing and getting stronger. Eventually, the new branches were bigger, stronger and more beautiful than the old ones. "Father, I said, thank you so much for healing me. I am stronger and more beautiful than ever. You are so good."

"Yes, my precious little tree, there are times we must replace what is weak by walking through the storm, trusting that you will become stronger if you always depend on me," he answered.

"Father, I said, thank you for creating me to be a tree. I will continue to be happy just being a tree."

3

My goodness, the weather has been unusual this year. Early spring brought a lot of rain and scary storms; then late spring and early summer it became very hot and dry which caused a drought. As far as I could see the grass was brown, flowers were dying, all of creation was suffering. Although I grew near a brook, it hardly had any water flowing and instead of being happy and bubbling, it was sad and barely moving. My leaves were drooping and my flowers falling off. I wondered how the creator's animals and people would survive if there wasn't any fruit to eat or water to drink.

I once again cried out to my father for help and answers. "Father," I asked, "have you forgotten us? Do you not see what is happening? Do you no longer love your creations? Everything is dying and drying up. Please help us!" "My precious little tree," he replied, "evil has invaded all that I have created, its goal is to destroy all that is good, by lying to all mankind. It has confused the minds of all people into thinking and acting in evil ways and not caring for this world or for each other. Your roots grow deep in the ground, tapping into the living water so you may live. You have always been faithful, obedient and thankful. There have been faithful people who love me. They have trusted and obeyed me, but at times some also have been deceived by evil. I am going to tell you a story that you need to hear, for your life's purpose is very near and I want you to understand when life seems darkest, that's when I'm about to do my best work for those who, like you, love me and have been faithful. I have chosen you to be more than just a tree. You will always be remembered, my precious little tree."

"Long ago when I created all that you see, I also created angels. They also each had individual purposes. Some messengers, others warriors, protectors, singers and worshipers. However, one very special angel who was very beautiful and powerful became full of pride and believed he was equal to his creator. His name was Lucifer. He deceived many other angels. They began to worship him. This behavior could not be tolerated in heaven. They had to be banned from heaven and were banished to earth. He is now called Satan or the Devil; his evil plan is to plant in the minds of all mankind to kill, steal and destroy all that I have created. This is now sin that consumes all mankind.

Just Be a Tree

To save mankind from their sin, there had to be a perfect sacrifice sufficient to free people from their sin. The only option was the perfect Lamb of God, my only Son, Jesus. He willingly left heaven to experience life on earth, and be an example of trusting and obeying the Father. This was accomplished through a very special young girl by the name of Mary, who loved the Father and had been obedient and faithful. An angel was sent to tell her the Father had chosen her to be the mother of Jesus. She was afraid because she was engaged to be married and thought he would turn his back on her, as well as her family and friends. However, she loved the Father and trusted him to take care of her; she obeyed and yielded herself to the Holy Spirit. The angel then went to Joseph, her fiancé, and told him that Mary was pregnant with the Son of God, and he should take her as his wife, trusting the Father to take care of them. Joseph also loved the Father, he obeyed and took Mary to be his wife, even though she was pregnant. When the time came, Jesus was born in a humble stable and would live on earth, for a short time, as the Son of Man and the Son of God.

Because of Mary's obedience, love and faith, she will be remembered for all eternity. My purpose for you, my precious little tree, will soon be accomplished and you also will suffer for a while, as my son will. I have chosen you for a very special purpose, for you have loved and trusted me. You also will be remembered for eternity."

It has been many years since the Father has shared his story with me and I sometimes wonder if my special purpose will actually take place. I have continued to be what He created me to be and have enjoyed being the best tree I can.

One day, which started out like any other, I saw some men coming toward me and as they got closer, I noticed they were carrying axes; they were coming to cut me down. I had seen this happen to other trees and thought it was horrible. When I asked my Father about it, he told me they were accomplishing his purpose and would be used in different, but very special ways, such as building a home, or furniture and other useful items. Others would be used to create beautiful art to be treasured always. I was so excited; I believe it is time for me to accomplish the very special purpose my Father had spoken of.

It hurt a lot when they started chopping into me, but I remembered that the Father had said I would suffer to carry out His purpose. They split me in two pieces and ripped all my bark off. I was in terrible pain, I thought I might die and that surely this had to be a mistake. "Father", I cried, please help me I think something is terribly wrong. I've been cut down, all my bark has been ripped off, I'm naked, ugly and in so much pain." He answered, "I know my precious little tree, I told you there would be much suffering, but it will be over soon. Know that I am with you and will walk through this pain with you. I will never leave you nor forsake you. You must believe this and trust me as you always have." "Yes, Father," I responded through my tears, "I will always believe and trust you. "

Just Be a Tree

The next thing they did was to cross one-piece over the other and nail them together. With each blow to the nail, I cried out in pain, but I could feel the presence of the Father with me. He said, "Be strong my precious little tree, it won't be much longer."

I was then dragged up a steep hill by a man who was beaten and bloody, he could hardly walk under the weight. At the top of the hill, he dropped me flat on the ground and other men threw him on top of me. They stretched his arms to each side of me and nailed his hands through his palms into me. They also nailed his feet together at the bottom of me and placed a crown of thorns on his head. I heard him cry out each time they struck the nails. I knew how much it hurt as it also hurt me. He hung there and I could feel his blood covering me.

As I looked around there was a large crowd, most were laughing, calling him names, even spitting on him. Some were calling him "The King of the Jews." Despite my pain, I felt honored to have a King hanging on me, but why would they be treating a King like this. I also heard some saying, "Why don't you save yourself". How could they think he could save himself? I also noticed one woman kneeling and crying. I heard her repeating "Jesus, Jesus, my son, I love you. This had to be Mary, the mother of Jesus. Now I know why she would be remembered for eternity.

I watched and listened in horror as this continued for a long time. "Father" are you still there, I asked? "I am," he replied. "Father, what is happening" I asked? "How could the people you created, and love be so cruel." He replied, "Evil has entered their minds and blackened their hearts". I asked, "Who is this man they have nailed to me who is hanging here bleeding, bruised, broken and barely alive?" My Father replied in a very broken, sad whisper, "This is my son Jesus, whom I told you of. He is the perfect Lamb of God, who is being slaughtered as the only sacrifice that is worthy to forgive mankind's sin. He is freely laying down his life to save the world." "His blood that has now saturated you, will cleanse those from sin, who repent and ask for my son, Jesus, to forgive them and be the Lord and Savior of their lives."

It was then the sky turned black as night, the wind blowing harder than I ever knew it could and there was an ear-shattering sound, the earth was shaking. Above all this I heard Jesus say in a loud voice, "My God, My God, why hast thou forsaken me!" Then as evening approached, Jesus cried out "It is finished" and he died. He was later taken down and carried away.

I was standing there alone, covered in the blood of Jesus, broken-hearted. "Father, I whispered, are you still there, I don't feel your presence with me." There was no response. All was silent.

5

I stood there for three long days, miserable, hurting and sad. I felt as if my Father had abandoned me. I prayed this was not so, as my father had promised he would never leave me.

On the third day, the sun shone brighter than I have ever seen it. Something had changed, it seemed like all creation was celebrating. I felt different somehow, strong, all my pain was gone, something had changed. I then heard my Father's voice speaking triumphantly. "My precious little tree, my Son, Jesus, has risen from the grave. He took upon himself the sin of the world. That is why I was silent. I could not look on the sin that He took upon himself**. With his death sin has been defeated and buried**. My son will now ascend back to heaven and sit at my right side, interceding for all those who come to the foot of the cross, repent of their sin, lay their burdens there, and ask Jesus to forgive them and ask Him to be Lord and Savior of their life. They will then be certain of the promise to live in heaven for eternity with the Father, Son and Holy Spirit.

"You, my precious little tree, have accomplished my purpose for you. You are that cross that bore the body of the Lamb of God, the Son of God, as he was dying, shedding his blood for all mankind, saturating your being with his cleansing blood, that those who humble themselves and kneel at the cross, will be cleansed by His blood."

"You will be known as the "Old Rugged Cross" forever."

"Father", I replied, "What a privilege and glorious honor it has been to be just a tree, fulfilling the purpose you created for me. I will stand here and gladly welcome all who come to the "Old Rugged Cross"

It wasn't the nails that held him there, but his love for you and me!

Author's Note

This is the first book I've ever written. I've never considered myself capable of writing a story. Well, God, had other plans. This all started with a Wednesday night bible study. I'm not sure of the exact nature of the specific study, but it involved hearing from God, God's plans for us and spiritual gifts. It became very deep and involved and invoked so many questions. I spent some time with God asking for his direction…I just didn't believe that it should be so complicated. God wants us to understand, and I believed it should be simple. He gave me an example of a tree, how it just does what it was created to be. I shared that with the group and that was the extent of it, or so I thought.

A couple of weeks later I had a dream about a tree. It was cute and funny, and I didn't give it much thought. A few weeks later, the Holy Spirit prompted me to write about the tree… I tried to ignore the voice, but it didn't let up. I sat down with paper and pen and said, "I don't have a clue how to write or what to say, if I'm to write something, you will have to give me the words. I sat for a few minutes in prayer and one sentence formed in my spirit. I wrote it down and just before I placed a period, another sentence came. This continued until the sentences quit coming. I then heard, "this is chapter One". There's a lot more involved in my story of what happened during the writing of this book, but it is rather long, so I will just say that over the next few months at unexpected times, I heard the Holy Spirit tell me it was time to write…one sentence at a time, one chapter at a time.

It was the most amazing event in my life. It has turned my life around to think that just like he used common people in the Bible as his vessels, He used me. It also made me realize that He had faith in me to know I would obey, trust, and take that first step of faith to write His story to share with the world for such a time as this. I never gave much thought to God trusting me to obey and having faith in me, it's always been me praying for the ability to trust, obey and having faith in him.

I would like to invite you to follow this link and listen to the song, "He Grew the Tree". I know it will be a blessing to you: https://www.youtube.com/watch?v=99CBs8XrMUg

You have a story.
We want to publish it.

Everyone has as a story to tell. It might be about something you know how to do, or what has happened in your life, or it may be a thrilling, or romantic, or intriguing, or heartwarming, or suspenseful story, starring a cast of characters that have been swimming around in your imagination.

And at Wyatt & Sons Publishers, we can get your story onto the pages of a book just like the one you are holding in your hand. With professional interior design and a custom, professionally designed cover built just for you from the start, you can finally see your dream of being an author become reality. Then, you will see your book listed with retailers all over the world as people are able to buy your book from wherever they are and have it delivered to their home or their e-reader.

So what are you waiting for? This is your time.

visit us at
www.wyattpublishing.com
for details on how to get started becoming a published author right away.

www.ingramcontent.com/pod-product-compliance
Lightning Source LLC
Chambersburg PA
CBHW041815040426
42451CB00001B/4